Spy Car

and Other Poems

Lynne Handy

Published by Push On Press

Spy Car and Other Poems - Copyright © 2015 by Lynne Handy
http://lynnehandy.com/

Cover design: William Pack (www.williampack.com)

Cover photo: Jeffrey Krabec

ISBN: 978-0692612330

"The emotion of art is impersonal. And the poet cannot reach this impersonality without surrendering himself wholly to the work to be done. And he is not likely to know that is to be done unless he lives in what is not merely the present, but the present moment of the past, unless he is conscious, not of what is dead, but of what is already living."

(T.S. Eliot, "Tradition and the Individual Talent," *Selected Essays of T.S. Eliot*, 1932)

To my daughter and life spirit, Morgan Murphy, who takes my hand
and guides me through it all.

I am especially grateful to Gloria Boyer for helping me grow as a poet and for editing most of the poems in this collection.

I'm also grateful to Jeffrey Krabec for photographing his MGB for the cover, to William Pack for designing the cover, and to Kevin Moriarity for formatting the chapbook for publication.

Contents

I

Statue of a Seated Boxer

Terme Boxer or Boxer of the Quirinal

The eyes are gone—
who knows if lost to thief or time.
When wrested from the Roman hill, the bronze was grimed;
no myrtle wreathed its massive head. The thewy form
was not upright in youthful prime, but resting on a rock,
older, spent, and wanting sleep.

Though the boxer's eyes are peerless,
it's not as if the sparrows pecked them out.
No, through some misadventure the marble orbs are gone,
but still the face bespeaks ordeals: the nose,
a mountain range worn flat; ears, molded lava pits;
and scars, riverine, chiseled.

Cheekbones like inlaid copper plains;
hair coiled and slicked with sweat beneath the Grecian sun;
beard smeared with blood; torso muscled like a bull;
legs like pylons, tendons tensed for yet another round;
manhood, infibulated; feet, broad; toes thick for balance,
for gripping ground.

Perhaps he was ready to throw his leathers in the ring.
Was this Virgil's old Entellus, who revived
to pound young Dares until the fight was stopped?
After smiting dead his prize, a golden bull, he cried,
Eryx, here I lay down my gauntlets and my art!

Ode to Floyd Mayweather, Jr.

To create a glorious life from your pain (Sophocles)

Floyd: his season.

     Unleash the panther man

       with tornadic twists

and metronomic pace.

     He whirs like a hornet, tenacity metered

in feints and punches. Pugnacity, controlled,

     and he likes those ropes

       so he can spring, curl,

     and shimmy down

to obfuscate opponents.

Birthmarked: a hustle past,

addict mom, boxer Pop selling drugs,

     pop pop of guns.

Story goes… dealer came to the crib,

out to kill Pop, who used baby Floyd as a shield.

     Normal was being passed around like a rock,

       Pop's hard fists, no male model

       except at the gym.

Punching bags, his best friends.

Escaped the crib with his fists and brain.

Pound for pound, greatest threat and pain.

Plotina at the Bridge

The restaurant is warm, the windows wide.
I sip tepid tea and gaze outside to see
Fox River in winterscape, waves aligned,
perfectly web-locked and rimmed with ice
in the sun's last blink—
miles of silver mail running south to big waters.

There is much to trouble a poet:
wars, superstition, and bigotry,
climate rot and misogyny.
A French writer invites a seventh-century world,
hurled forward to squelch marketplace sex
and save the family, a task requiring
multiple wives chained like riverine mail.

Focusing on the bridge near State Street,
a thigh-high structure astride bow-legged pylons—
a headless, armless Trajan straddling the Danube,
waterway of caesars and kings—I think of Trajan's wife
Plotina, who understood
peaceful minds come from calm living
and absence of pain.
But who ever heard of her?

Eve in Bosch's *The Garden of Earthly Delights*

A seed flambés and pops into a pod: it is my brain awakening.
Four limbs telescope from my trunk, and breeding organs pipe
pink above my viscera. Beneath my chin, a dairy bar opens.
I burst bent from bone.

I am not born, nor am I made of dust. No one breathes the soul
of life into my nostrils. I slide out beneath a fetid armpit
to lie aground, facing Rock Face, he of carapaced eye
and blacksnake moustache.

Upon rising, my eyes fall on a cesspool filled with vermin
and birds, some free and good, and some encrusted with pearly lies
formed from a sand speck that so plagued an oyster, he blew his nacre.
I would have run away … but where?

A sleeping form bestirs, yawns, sits up, and upon seeing a gash
in its side, bleats long and loud. Then from a pink monstrance
where the Eucharist is kept steps a godlike figure with butter curls,
and robed in robin's tongue pink.

The form's screams rattle the scalloped hills the arid sky the blue lake
and the god wiggles his fingers to heal him. Then the form stretches out
in a puppy dog way to graze god's foot .. god grips my wrist
and tells him—this—

this place, including me, is his dominion. I'm miffed.
A murky pool beckons, a way to grow aslant with knowledge seeded,
to be a fish with wings, a bird with three heads, a missile piercing the sky
with its beak. I howl at the moon like a crocoboon.

Epithalamion (Wedding Song)

I, Havier, bear pyracantha on my antlers
to celebrate the wedding of my friend,
the noble West Wind, to the Snow Maiden,
who shivers in the cumulus of his breath.
Let me tell you how he cooled my pelt
in summer's heat and warned me
with frigid blasts to winter in the glen.
He swathed my hide with chilly drafts
to soothe my melancholic mind.

For eons, he preserved my ilk,
sank seeds into the soil and paused
the shafted sun to warm the earth,
to root and leave the understory;
and breezed the forest trees, giving
to the greening of the land. I weep;
swallow twice in gratitude, and laud
his croonings, great and small.
His crystalline reward: his rimy bride.

He, tactician of shifts, is amenable
to change. Suitor no longer,
true husband to the snow,
and she no longer lone, but strewn
through union with the force that merges
her and him into hieroglyphic shapes,
their progeny, to scatter over lakes and land
and drape the window panes with tinseled flakes.

Klimt Morning

He paints with rain
on screen mesh

a goddess wearing raindrops
like silver sequins.

Tears from a thousand eyes
glint down wooden shingles

to pool near the drain spout,
a Niagara gush,

gathered from gutters
to water the silver mums.

Something Like a Sonnet for Lucie Brock-Broido

She buckles on her rusty belt, when she leaves for New York
And feels in her Bones and bee-lined bonnet, the primal grit
Of smokestacks and bridges, as she lifts her pen to torque
A primer for divining spells, and Using gentle wit,
Illuminates, writing of California and Carrowmore,
Where blooming grapes and gangs and bones all have a say.
Odes corrode, erupt in sadness, yet demand the awful spore
Of wonder, a boost to bolt among the tombs for one more day.
Pennant poised, she pleads for Took, a founding Crip,
An altered man redreamed, rethemed, by literary success.
Arnold flips the switch and she translates Tookie's trip
To his blue purlieu in terms that shame, enflame, possess.
Her muse lives not in gardens, but in down-and-dirty news.
Sweet mystic of pain and plain, she myth-makes and construes.

Midnight Walk by the River

---after Carl Sandburg

Up timber planks I climb to the
bridge where the cool plaque of fog
comes
spilling over the water on
a black night. I sit on a little
bench and what might be a cat
runs out to chew on my feet.

I yelp for help, leap up, and smack it
with my umbrella; it runs away, sits
under a flickering lamp, looking
not like a cat, but a hound, and over-
weight, at that. Showing I harbor
no ill will, I speak kindly and
leave, walking west, toward the city.
The dog comes, his toenails clatter on
the bridge, a jazzy patter. No longer silent,
night comes alive. Dog disappears. On haunches,
I search under benches, stare into the river trench. Then
memories of love sadden me. Something moves
closer, finds me, licks me, loves me. It and I go on.

Blue Ribbons for Kizzy

Lyrical essay remembering Keziah Ann Poyner Handy and her descendants

Kizzy loves the sea, sky and swamplands. In 1836 when she is thirteen, her family leaves worn-out North Carolina soil to find fertile land. With folks from the Mt. Zion United Methodist Church, they head northwest in four creaking wagons and three carts, jingling bells on the horses's collars. They bump over trails, singing hymns as pure as blue mountain air, and chart stars like cutouts on Mammy's pies. Flanked by forests, their ears thrill to the whisper of leaves, the chirr of wrens and cackle of crows. They love the red cardinal's wing that teases like kisses through canopied branches. At nightfall, woodland creatures screech. Women, children lie quiet in the wagons; men keep muskets close to their gun hands.

They settle in Indiana near the Wabash, north of the National Road. Cabin squats on black earth sacred to Kizzy's pa. He grows corn tall as sunflowers and wheat that flashes gold in the sun, but life is hard. Momma's hands roughen like burlap as she scrubs clothes on a washboard and cuts up rabbits for the firepot.

Kizzy works hard too, but carries longing in her bones, tied up with blue ribbons. She misses the roar of blue sea, the bite of salt air, the whinny of horses running wild on beaches, the sweep of sea oats on windy days, and the heat that drooled sweat down her back like wooly-worms. She misses the Negro girl, filling her bath with warm water and the boy who washed the verandah clean of bird droppings. She misses cries from the swamp, old granny spinning tales of the war—the Fox and his men hiding behind cypress knees.

She is sixteen when her eyes light on James Handy, a young farmer, whose family hails from New York. Etched with smile lines, his face favors a good-natured soul and he loves the river changes like she adored the moods of the sea. They wed while blue fingers of ice still grip the meadow. Children come—Thomas, Alfred, the girls, and little John. From James's side, strong Dutch blood flows in their veins and they thrive like the crops; they are beautiful like the sea.

Industry teems in the little river towns: farm yields are plentiful; packets and steamboats float grain up-and-down-river; teamsters haul goods via the National Road— the clip clop of six-horse teams is steady, like the tick of a clock. But gray clouds are piling behind southern hills. In meeting places, men debate slavery. Is it God's intent that men should own men? No, say some. Others believe in Noah's prophecy *Read Genesis 9*, they say. *It's all because Ham looked on old Noah's nakedness.* Pro-Union politicians note the state is heavily seeded with southerners. Kizzy has feet on both sides of the Mason-Dixon Line and fears for her sons.

Three weeks after Christ rises from the dead, war erupts at a sea fort. James looks Kizzy and her kin in the eye and denounces the South. Son Thomas dons the Union blue and marches off to the front. A Carolina cousin writes that her own boys, clad in gray, have gone off belching fire. Nary a day goes by that Kizzy doesn't send up a prayer for somebody.

Her nerves rattle; she can't bear that God's grassy pastures and timbered woods are battlefields and her boy, who has the starry-eyed look of a dreamer, is soldiering. Days, months pass. Then word of Thomas's death comes on a November day when snow spatters fields like cotton tufts. Measles! He died of measles. Had he been home, she could have nursed him to health! Kizzy groans at the loss of her firstborn, grabs a butcher knife, and cuts her hair ragged. James swears to bring their boy home, to lay him beneath the maple where his grandparents lie.

In the east, a blizzard rages like a monster of yore; James rides into its devil core to retrieve his son's body. Three hundred and fifty miles. He goes alone with a wagon and team. Over frozen trails he heads south into the neutral state, Kentucky. He urges the horses up steep hills, down icy slopes; he gets out, pushes the wagon. His clothes are soaked. Inns are few. Cold, wet, his beard frozen, his belly empty, he presses on. Eleven days it takes to reach Columbus to fetch his boy's corpse. Then back with his load, more precious than rubies. Up, down, the sun is shining now, the snow melting, not so cold as before. The horses slush through washouts. Up, down. Then home. James comes home ill. Kizzy makes broth to strengthen him. Second son Alfred digs his brother's grave and the Methodists say words. James dies before spring planting.

Kizzy is a godly woman, but James passing so soon after Thomas devastates her. Like the fig tree, she dries up. No Bible verse spoken by her preacher brother moves her. There's the land to farm, a house to build, children to feed, but she takes to her bed, dreaming of blue waters, horses splendid in the sun, and the hot breath of trees when they catch wind fever.

The girls run the household, care for their small brother. With the help of neighbors, Alfred finishes building the new house and farms the land. He sees to the marrying of his sisters and Kizzy's burying when the time comes. Later, he marries, sires ten proud children, one of them named Kizzy, who is no dreamer, but a practical school teacher with wild curly hair and painful bunions in old age.

II

Melange

Old fiddle wind strums doodah
bawdy firs
        kick high,
                flash thigh
dead leaves scat—
        half-notes on a staff.
wake up, cymbal moon,
                    and crash.

dawn's orange-throated trumpet
                        blares
while clefted pears strain
        against chains
lily pods hit high C
        and ivy fists loosen their
clench on the fence.

bebop jump
        con
          fusion!
        the felonious sun
        pedals into a cloud bank
and riffs new notes
        for the day.
Who'll tell?
        Tiger lily: *Not me.*

The Cup

When Mary poured the wine
and bore the cup to Christ,
she heard his words:
This is my blood.
Up cup to hold and down to spill, which later
came amid deceptions, his mother's wail,
the frenzy of friends, and the figment of his flesh.

The cup, its *wholiness* with space and sides,
held all required to save the human race,
and lent itself to legends—
Arthurian tales about the grail and knights
who wore their deeds like silver mail.

Few symbols live from days gone by—
takes too long to think them through
or know their provenance—or care.
Now folks prefer emblazonings
that appear and disappear—
like the ingrown toenail
encased in a purple helmet
shown on TV last night.

November Study

Weather prediction: morning sun,
giving way to clouds. Wind grabs
my throat with frozen claw.

I slog in leaves up to my shins.
On a side street, my eyes come alive:
red car, saluki snout parked in a drive
under bright yellow trees.

Between two fences dried stalks bear
ears of Indian corn; a brown squirrel appears,
drops a ruby red kernel in the slumbering grass.

But hear the withering of the plants,
the death rattle—

they have fallen in their traces
and won't rise again.

Hybrid Images of Marilyn and Albert

She slips through time with droopy eyes
and donut lips and hour-glass hips.
He found the key to relativity;
hence, therefrom: the atom bomb.

Superimposed by MIT
their faces seem to merge.
The far-sighted will see Marilyn,
while the near-sighted find Albert.
Take a look. Up close—it's he.
Now stand back. You'll see it's she.

The algorithm paired their faces—
It was their mournful eyes, I'll bet:
she hated being a bombshell,
and he regretted abetting the bomb.

Our Monkey Selves

We loll in treetops,
make *muh-muh* sounds,
and throw stones at God's own clones,
scrambling down below.

Plop. One stone wastes a man
known for base intents;
he lost his life just before
an ambulance arrived.
Plop. That rock struck dead
a boy embedded in a
pure white soul. *Plop plop.*
It took two hurls
to clock a girl running fast
beside an underpass.

The randomness of rocks
thrown by monkey paws—
seems explained
by carelessness.
Their paws
so like our own—

The Polemics of Bees

In the violet tint of afternoon, my asters curl their leaves and lure me out of doors. Purple-blossomed, gussied up with greening stems, they cry: *Come, come and see!* I hurry down the steps, cross the lawn, then stop. Feasting on my flowers is a grit of bees, thirty or more, toy-like in their black and yellow rompers—Beatrix Potter's Babbity Bumbles, who hived in Mrs. Tittlemouse's house till she tore out their nest and rigged her door so only mice could enter. Still she bought wax from the bees, and honey…

This damson day I back away. My trapezii tense, mandible clenches, nares flare. Driven from my garden by uninvited guests, and worse, ones whose sting I fear. The bees are immigrants (they do not *live* in my yard), taking pollen where they can. I did not ask them in, but they are here, in their place in the universe, as with my own stock, English farmers and herders, who centuries ago crossed an ocean to seize a land so their progeny could flower…just as people cross borders now with the grit of life between their teeth.

Storm Front

Clouds drape, take anvil shape.
Rain bites the window with little teeth.
We wait—
      for government staff to leap to life.
In this room, tension builds, unsparked—
old men, old women, Latinas with wailing niños,
all parked on chairs sagging from the drag
of their no-bodies.

All eyes align on the clock. At nine
windows grind open and closed faces appear.
A door unleashes a polyestered woman,
screaming at a Latina: *You should learn English!*
A baby shrieks, a primal, gut-slamming cry.
An old woman shakes awake, a man racks out a cough,
a toddler looks out the window and slaps his brother,
afraid of the coming storm.

Doodling Zeus

black bully clouds stalk the sunshine
zeus rumbles at his children
and scratches imprecations
on the skyboard with golden fingernails

Blue Windmill Blues

Rebel at fifty, embittered man,
tilts at blue fractals,
an alien clan, invading black fields
once yielding crops, now, used, abused,
scarred terrain ginning power from Hoosier winds.
Farmers sign contracts for six thousand a pop.

Each blighted day, those devil blue blades
dance the wing-wang sublimely,
out of step, out of time, and drone away birdsong
with high tech scat and a backbeat of groan.
Whirs and pings and tingle-down zats   spit
wintricity to faraway grids.

Burn Rebel Man, for the thrill
of peckerwoods drilling on oak;
the swish-swash of reeds as deer pass by creeks;
the crushed hush of leaves on prairie-grown trees,
wing trails of eagles, huzz-buzz of bees, the repertoire
of lost whippoorwill choirs—

Rebel Man has an ear for freedom
and he heard its last gasp
when he half-opened his door and saw windmills
goin' up fast on his neighbor's field. He nuzzles his dog,
lets out a slow moan, then comforts his suffering
with weed, homegrown.

III

Prints in the Snow

One foot is toed, one fingered.
Two pawed with sharp dew claws.
Two legs are fuzzed with fur; an arm, a sleek-skinned leg.
All mine.

I am half dog, half human.
My face-form is beast,
a plume-y hound-head with fallen ears
and cold wet nose, my torso, hirsute.
My woman-sex, one arm and leg are human.

I am dog-witted and human-kenned.
I catch the scent of carrion from miles away,
hear canaries sneeze, and dew weep from the leaves.
At dawn or dusk, my eyes spot distant foxes.
My paw-pads dowse, feel the earth-core rumple.

In rutting season, I flee from dog and man.
Dogs hump and wander on.
But men.
Those devils pump and hoot, then thrash me with their boots.

But I have freedoms—
running with packs, treeing cats, howling at red-gashed moons.
I lap through secret meadows,
my ears feathering like sister angel wings.

A Bluebeard Fable

The duke's small son killed helpless forest creatures, using hand-made traps that severed their extremities with a precision unusual in the eleventh century. At age ten, he galloped his pony to behead lone travelers who strayed into the ducal woods. As he matured, bluey hairs extruded from his peachy cheeks, then foliated into a cobalt bush. Townsmen referred to him as Bluebeard—Blu, for short.

At Acre, the old duke laid down his life for Jesus. Blu interrupted his depravities to bade the abbe say a mass. Soon he wed a countess whose coital cry-outs soothed his sexual predilections, but when she conceived an heir, she disdained their maiming games and demanded rest. Wild for her screams, Blu laid upon her knife-nicks until she begged God to take her and He did. Blu then skinned her corpse—her empty dermis reminded him of moths that flew atop the keep. He fed her to the hogs and swung her casing from a hook, liking the look of an empty cocoon.

Next Blu wed a baroness, a duchess, a princess of the realm. He adored their clamor, but when seeded they stilled as the countess had, and he dispatched them to the Lord.

A shepherdess, Georgine, by name, caught his eye—or ear—as she shrilled at her sheep. Georges, her twin, warned of Blu's fiendish reputation, but she ignored him. *Mind thy own business*, she hissed. She had warmed to Blu's kisses as a cinder bites a log. On a gray day in May, she wed him, shared his eider down bed, amused him with bawdy tales and ear-splitting yodels, and did not mind his jabs and bites and nerve-racking chases through the castle. But then, as a child began to grow inside her womb, her ardor cooled—she began to nest.

Not long after, Blu stabbed her.

Miles away, Georges felt the blade gore his soul. Yanking his horse around, he raced up the hill and crossed the moat, his horse's hooves clattering novenas on the timbered bridge. An open door revealed his sister's ashen sac suspended from a silver nail. Georges stalked Blu through moth-winged halls and slew him; then bore the corpse to the pig lot, where the sows, slopping happily in the mud, had not yet devoured Georgine. Threading her into her casing, he carried her off and revived her at their mother's cottage.

Blu? It was the end of him. Georgine's child? It survived, and its progeny may be seen tilling the foothills near Beaune to this day.

It Happened in the Night

Squint-eyed Jack built his hut
atop a faerie fort,
not heeding circle ridges;
nor did he note the Druid dolmen
mid gorse and thorns.

Neighbors told him
faerie folk would seek revenge,
but fearless Jack closed both ears
and moved to the faerie sphere
with wife and newborn child.

The wife had shimmery locks
and wild rose lips, and was unsure
who sired her son. Jack?
Or the devil, which appeared
one night in silver form
with long-lobed ears, curly tail,
and templed horns.

A fortnight passed. Plain to see—
Baby favored neither Jack nor she—
in fact, he had a silver sheen,
a bobby tail, and nubbins on his head.
She shaved his temples
and when Jack asked about the bloody stumps,
"*It happened in the night,*" she said.
"*Faeries took them for the rent.*"
Each month, poor baby creature
lost a feature—his long-lobed ears, his tail...
"*It happened in the night,*" said Mum. "*Rent again.*"

But Baby's silvery skin—what was she to do?
There seemed no way to bleach it peach,

so she took aim, pitched him off a cliff,
and claimed the faeries took him.

One crone-moon night, the shack
teetered back and forth.
When Jack and wife spilt out,
faeries peppered them with elf-shot
and flung them in the sea.
"To hell with you," they yelled,
"for breaching our demesne!"
And Baby?
Faeries had picked him from the ditch
and restored his missing parts.
On a lily-petal litter, they bore him to the fort
and found him parents in the netherworld
who loved him well and good.

Bloody Mary: A Divining Ritual

Bloody Mary, Bloody Mary, Bloody Mary,
Reveal the man whom I will marry …

In snare of night, she ascends
backward: heels stamping on the stairs,
candlestick clenched in left hand,
brass looking-glass in her right.
Bloody Mary: she thrice invokes
a papist queen who burnt dissenters
at the stake, now soothsayer in a game
to conjure up a lover.

Flames rise high and walls
reflect roasting fires.
Shadows rear, but no face appears.
Poignant, a girl's disappointment;
her lower lip protrudes, tears leach
down her cheeks; her soft chin
trembles like a petal in a breeze.
Does no one seek her love?

Then, she looks in the mirror …
a fine nose appears, a jaw
bold and strong, eyes the shade
of an angry sea, hair like a misted sun,
chest rippled and hard, his manhood
hale, legs, two muscled shanks,
and strong arms to brace, embrace.
This gilded god, all hers!

The candle sparks out.
She holds the cold glass on the darkened stairs.

IV

Girl Finding Voice

Sometimes I sleep
near ghosts in petal-dried rooms
where I can't sense my father's rage.

I am like him, Mother says,
but I think not.
She mistakes form for content.

Give me a balloon,
lift me above the cornsilks.
Show me gypsy wagons

and wooden crosses leaning left.
Let me bite into boulders
and skyscraper stones.

I hear fireflies,
smell sweet alyssum on my tongue,
taste Longfellow's *Hesperus*.

Let me dream and hear my little sister sing.
Crush the roses on my brother's grave.
Each day forward is a broken link.

Witness

papa pillared
like Trajan's bridge
in grandma's parlor
thundering at mama
who bleeds for understanding
because a house
is burning down the street
she's sorry sorry sorry
for her tears, her fears,
for the fire she set a month ago
hatching duck eggs in the house
and for the dead son she bore him
last year
and that she lives
still.

The Sellout

Seated in a side pew,
Mother darts her eyes
and cores my brainpan
like a Pippin.

I'd implored her not to make me lie.
It's my soul that will be judged, I'd cried.
She hadn't blinked. *What would Grandma think?*

The pastor leads the Creed.
The hour of sinning is upon me
and words drip like soured cider from my lips.
I believe...

So many wrongs—
the lie, her threats,
the pastor's putdown
that I was too unlearned
to know the way.
Rage still roars like hellfire.
I lacked a spine to stand my ground that day.

Sister Dream

In a bluish haze, she came to my tower,
arrayed in gray with modish shoulder pads,
gripping the hands of boy and girl,
and to her right, a shadow man
grazed the blue-tinged wall.

I was in a winding sheet, yet unwound,
the tail plunging past my feet,
a white rhino
crashing down into a pool,
and splashing up blue geysers of dust,
then drifting to a bouncy floor
where, in a corner, my father frolicked innocently
with giggling children.

In life, she had been the amusing one,
but in the dream, it was I tripping ridiculously,
barefoot, half-dressed, running a gas-fired vehicle
that stretched so I could lift her and her companions
to the tower's second tier. Though I ached to speak to her,
I was of no more consequence than an elevator.

School Friend

She was heroic for tromping on her white dress
in Home Ec class because she'd had to rip out her zipper
too many flipping times (didn't we all want to scream?).
And yes, once she peed on the floor when a teacher forbade us
to go to the restroom. She had auburn hair, pale skin with chicken pox
scars, the lidded eyes of a Spanish saint and a droll wit.

She had secrets and years afterward, I remembered
when her father had looked at me, my skin shrank into my clothes.

What I Did Yesterday

7AM: Woke to alarm and dove deep into the eiderdown. Lifted my head, found Adam's linen pillow smooth as an icy pond. Heart banging in my ribby cage, fed breakfast to kids and walked them to their bus. *Mental note: croquet equipment scattered amid fallen leaves, put away for spring.*

10AM: Adam straggled in, spent rooster, limp coxcomb. Whiskey-soured, he showered, left for work in three-piece worsted and silken tie. Smelled woman scent on his undershirt and shorts, watched water flow onto his jizzy clothes, lowered the washer lid. Time spun dry.

4PM: Kids came home; treated them to honey crisps, then we stacked the croquet set near the back porch and brought out a rake and mini-rakes to hustle leaves into dusty heaps.

7PM: Adam, home, jovial mood, brought yellow roses. Ice chimed inside his highball glass as I ringed my steak ragout with saffron rice and blue cheese biscuits.

9PM: Read to kids, kissed them, and slipped outside to steal the moon. Red leaf fell onto my hair. I felt its blow. Adam stumbled out, called my name, a profanity spoken with his breath. I struck him with a mallet and like a fallen buck, he sprawled onto a pile of leaves.

3AM: Heard him unlatch the door and later found him stretched out on the sofa, a bloody bruise spreading on his jaw. Covered him with his mother's afghan.

Door

A wreath raked with frost,
a door armed to repel the hoary eye
of winter
>   The grit of loss still grinds against
>   my softer parts.
>   I've thought of dying

Why not? There's the gas oven, like Plath
>   I could choose that path or pills like Teasdale
>   or Crane's leap in the sea—

Out there a snowed-over hell
in me too, in lieu
of living.

March: whitetail deer approach
on horn-tipped hooves,
feed on acorns by the porch

My blood pulses through clots of ice,
>   warms—
>   I fear leaving myself and
hear
the birds of spring appear and
I am nearer the door. Do I
>   design a new self—
>   one more inclined to—

but leaving me would grieve me

Parkin' Lot Cowboys

midnight
hangdog moon
lanky, lunky cowboys
slouched against
a pickup truck,
drinkin' beer
howlin'
to Waylon's mournful tunes.

Sun-Dried Tomatoes in a Beauty Salon

A woman entered the salon,
champagne colored hair,
end-flipped at her shoulders,
wearing apple-green pants
and peach-toned boots.
Borne on a westerly wind
she came from the Petroleum Club,
streaming tales of grasshopper wells run dry,
and of her menfolk, the wildest wildcatters
of them all.

She carried a two-gallon glass boot,
spiggoted, filled with vodka,
sun-dried tomatoes, and one-eyed olives
that stared out like guppies at tin-foiled ladies
with cheeks creased by love and pain,
listening to the stories,
remembering their own—
when life powered through their veins:
black gold through the North Texas pipeline.

The Whistler

Inside Walmart,
next to yellow bags of bird seed,
an old man sits on a bench,
whistling in a minor key.

Without warning, the earth dips,
and I lean into the tune. My self ignites
as my feet beat a slow clog
on a twisting trail.

I pause, hear the rush of wings flying home.
Ancient vines bind my feet
and I want to stay in this blooded place
where my bones are taking root,

but it doesn't last,
can't last—
the damp leaves, the sod, can't blot out the singe
of hotdogs roasting on spits
and voices shrilling to five dollar T-shirts.

Circle Game

Your lips touched my mind
as you traveled my orbit.
Bird hair, you once said,
meaning feathers.
You, city tiger,
crawling through alleys
smelling Tupac's rose
among the molt.
What is in the cup?
You and I—we don't explain.
We are circle players.

Poet's Breakfast

the toaster's breath
warms my fingers
as I pull a gluten-free disc from its slot,
and lift a knife to smear its pitted face
with a cholesterol-reduced spread from Finland,
purchased from a grocery fifteen miles away,
and crunchy almond butter from Trader Joe's,
which is nearer.
I pour wild blueberries in a bowl
and brew a mug of tea
smug   that I have thinned
my blood, tanked up on protein,
and awakened my synapses
with enough flavonoid
to last me through the morning.

Now if only I walked six miles daily
like my sister with the artificial knee.

Spy Car

The little car had lost its spiff.
Lifting off its tarp, it thumbed a tow
to my grandson's garage where he replaced
the brakes, ignition, clutch hydraulics,
pumps, belts, hoses, and the choke.
It's bracken chassis overhauled,
the vintage MGB positively preened:
an orange Saluki, revved and ready for the road.

Day after the blood moon fired the sky,
we went, top down, for a ride.
He concentrated on engine sounds, hums
and spits and thrums, as we flashed past
cornfields, woods, feeling the lash
of wind, listening as the car spoke,
he in tattersall cap, and I
in checkered cloak and billowing scarf.

(Remember *Man with the Golden Gun?*
Agent 007 hitched a ride in a 73
MGB from Hong Kong harbor.)
My grandson and I sit low in leather seats,
sweeping along Illinois highways,
eyes riveted through a shared windshield
on the unspooling road ahead.

Notes

I

Statue of a Seated Boxer was inspired by a photo of a statue of the same name discovered on Rome's Quirinal Hill by archaeologist Rodolfo Lanciani in 1885. The statue was dated third century BCE.

Ode to Floyd Mayweather, Jr celebrates the boxing career of Mayweather. The poem was written soon after his fight with Manny Pacquiao in 2015.

Plotina at the Bridge is a meditation that took place at a family restaurant overlooking the Fox River in North Aurora, Illinois. Emperor Trajan lived 53-117 CE. He ruled the Roman Empire 98-117 CE and commissioned an arched bridge to be built over the Danube River.

Eve in Bosch's *The Garden of Earthly Delights* was inspired by Hieronymus Bosch's (1450-1516) triptych altarpiece. As Bosch did not date his paintings, he would have painted the triptych between 1490 and 1510.

Epithalamion (Wedding Song) was the result of an exercise from an online course taught by J. Carlo Matos. An epithalamion is the best man's toast to the bride and groom.

Klimt Morning was inspired by lighting and rain drops collecting on a window screen conjuring up paintings by Gustave Klimt (1862-1918).

Something Like a Sonnet for Lucie Brock-Broido was inspired by the elliptical poetry of Lucie Brock-Broido (1956-   ).

Midnight Walk by the River is written in the *golden shovel* form, introduced by National Book Award-winning poet Terrance Hayes. Read downward, the final word of each line comprises a poem by another poet. In *Midnight Walk by the River* the imitated poem is *Fog* by Carl Sandburg (1878-1967).

Blue Ribbons for Kizzy was inspired by the life of Keziah Ann Poyner Handy (1823-1896), the poet's great-great-grandmother.

II

Melange formed in the poet's mind while watching a storm pass through the back yard in Champaign, Illinois.

The Cup is a bow to Arthurian legend, but with a modern twist.

November Study is the result of a late autumn walk through a North Aurora, Illinois neighborhood.

Hybrid Images of Marilyn and Albert was inspired by the hybrid optical illusion created by neuroscientists at Massachusetts Institute of Technology.

Our Monkey Selves came to mind watching the movement of trees and reflecting on mankind.

The Polemics of Bees was the result of an exercise from an online course taught by J. Carlo Matos in which the poet composed and edited a poem in view of others.

Storm Front was inspired by people in the waiting room of a Texas social security office.

Doodling Zeus is the result of watching lightning in a Midwestern summer storm.

Blue Windmill Blues was inspired by the wind turbines covering the landscape of Benton County, Indiana. Benton County has wind speeds similar to those around Lake Michigan, and was the first county in Indiana to host wind turbines. The first commercial operation began in 2008. Although windfarms add to the local economy, people voice concerns about decreased property values, increased noise levels, and disturbance to wildlife. (*Benton County, Indiana Website*)

III

Prints in the Snow is the result of an assignment to create a poem about a half-human, half-beast character.

A Bluebeard Fable was inspired by *Bluebeard*, a French folktale. Charles Perrault recorded eight folktales, told to him by his peasant nurse, into literary form in *Histoires ou Contes du temps passé; avec des Moralitéz*. The book was published by Barbin in Paris in 1697. The other folktales were *La Belle au Bois Dormant* (The Sleeping Beauty), *La Petit Chaperon Rouge* (Little Red

Riding Hood), *Le Maistre Chat, ou le Chat Botte* (Puss in Boots), Les Fées, (Diamonds and Toads), *Cendrillon, ou la petite Pantoufle de Verre* (Cinderella or The Glass Slipper), Riquet à la Houppe (Riquet with the Tuft), and *Le Petit Poucet* (Hop o' my Thumb). (*Children's Books in England*, Harvey Darton).

It Happened in the Night was the result of an effort to write an original magical realism poem using faeries as the rescuers. According to the *Dictionary of Celtic Mythology*, faeries may be clever, mischievous, and capable of assisting or harassing human behavior.

Bloody Mary Divining Ritual was created after reading about many of the divining rituals people use in games. Many of the earliest rituals regarding mirrors and divination originated in the British Isles.

IV

Girl Finding Voice references the schooner *Hesperus* in Henry Wadsworth Longfellow's poem "The Wreck of the *Hesperus*", published in *Ballads and Other Poems* in 1842.

Witness references Trajan's Bridge (Bridge of Apollodorus), built in 105 CE by Emperor Trajan (reigned 98-117 CE) in present-day Serbia to guarantee supply lines for Roman legions quartered in conquered Dacia. The engineer Apollodorus of Damascus used wooden arches. The bridge's spans were the longest built for more than one thousand years (Encyclopedia Britannica).

The Sellout references the Apostles Creed, an early statement of Christian belief. Date of origin not known. Purported at one time to be a creed composed by the twelve disciples of Jesus Christ, and later from separate writings of the New Testament. (*Catholic Encyclopedia*)

Sister Dream is composed of dream images.

School Friend includes "the lidded eyes of a Spanish saint," a nod to the paintings of El Greco (Domenikos Theotokopoulos, 1541-1614), architect of the Spanish Renaissance.

What I Did Yesterday is a first effort on the part of the poet to write a lyrical essay.

Door references poets Sylvia Plath (1932-1963), Sara Teasdale (1884-1933), and Hart Crane (1899-1932). All took their own lives.

Parkin' Lot Cowboys was written in Fort Worth, Texas.

Sundried Tomatoes in a Beauty Salon was inspired by regular customers in a Fort Worth, Texas beauty salon.

The Whistler was inspired by a trip to a downstate Illinois Walmart.

Circle Game includes "smelling Tupac's rose among the molt." The estate of rapper/poet Tupac Shakur (1971-1996) published *The Rose that Grew from Concrete*, a collection of his poems, in 1999.

Poet's Breakfast refers to Benecol, "a cholesterol-reduced spread from Finland," and Trader Joe's, an American privately-held chain of specialty grocery stores based in California.

Spy Car was inspired by a ride in a MGB, owned by Jeffrey Krabec. The MGB is a two-door sports car manufactured by the British Motor Corporation, later British Leyland, as a four-cylinder soft top roadster from 1962-1980. In *Man with a Golden Gun*, a James Bond film, actress Britt Eklund, portraying Bond's Hong Kong contact, Mary Goodnight, drives a harvest gold RHD MGB. She picks up Bond at the Star Ferry pier and drives him to the Peninsula Hotel.

Acknowledgments

Eve in Bosch's *The Garden of Earthly Delights*, *Clementine Poetry Journal*, November, 2015

Melange, *Clementine Poetry Journal*, May, 2015

Doodling Zeus, *Clementine Poetry Journal*, January, 2015

Blue Windmill Blues, *Pegasus*, Winter/Spring 2013

School Friend, *Clementine Poetry Journal*, October, 2015

Door, *Pegasus*, Winter/Spring, 2015

The Whistler, *Pegasus*, Summer/Autumn, 2015